Weathering and Erosion

Weathering and Erosion

Text by Christina Wilsdon

Photography: Cover, p. 1, CORBIS; pp. 3, 4 top, 24, Siede Preis/Photodisc; p. 4 bottom, Tim McGuire/CORBIS; p. 5, Lester Lefkowitz/CORBIS; p. 6, Edmund Van Hoorick/Photodisc; p. 7 top, Ray Michaud/Four Lakes Colorgraphics Inc.; p. 7 bottom, John Wang/Photodisc; pp. 8, 18, Ron Watts/CORBIS; pp. 9 left, 19, Galen Rowell/CORBIS; pp. 9 right, 14, 18-19, Photodisc; p. 10, David Muench/CORBIS; pp. 11, 15, Robert Glusic/Photodisc; pp. 12 top, 13, 16, 21, CORBIS; p. 12 bottom, Tom Bean/CORBIS; p. 17, Paul A. Sounders/CORBIS; p. 20, Pat O'Hara/CORBIS; pp. 22-23, Reuters NewMedia Inc./CORBIS.

Literacy Consultant: Phoebe Bell Ingraham, Reading Recovery Teacher Leader, Wright State University

Literacy Teacher Advisors: Mona Bailey, Reading Specialist, Title I Coordinator; Amy Bodey, Reading Specialist; Samentha Lucas, Reading Specialist; Jessica McCombe, Reading Specialist

Reviewer: Michael Grote, Ed.D., Math and Science Education

Developed by Four Lakes Colorgraphics Inc. in cooperation with Zaner-Bloser, Inc.

ISBN: 0-7367-1909-1

Copyright © Zaner-Bloser, Inc.

All rights reserved. No part of this book may be reproduced or transmitted in any form or by any means, electronic or mechanical, including photocopying, recording, or by any information storage and retrieval system, without permission in writing from the Publisher.

Zaner-Bloser, Inc., P.O. Box 16764, Columbus, Ohio 43216-6764, 1-800-421-3018

Printed in China

03 04 05 06 07 (133) 5 4 3 2 1

Table of Contents

Hard as Rock

Pick up a rock.
Hold it in your hand.
How does it feel?
Is it smooth and round?
Is it rough and jagged?
Is it heavy?
Can you break it by dropping
it on another rock?

Most rocks are very hard. We need machines to break hard rock into smaller pieces. Sometimes dynamite is used to shatter a big rock to bits.

These rocks are so strong and hard that we can use them to build buildings, roads, and statues. Earth itself is made out of rock.

Mount Rushmore, South Dakota

Weathering

Special machines can break down rock. Do you think water can also break down rock? What about ice? Can a plant split a rock? What about wind? Can chemicals crumble rock, too?

Believe it or not—they can!

Water, ice, plants, wind, and chemicals can all help break down rock. This breaking down is called **weathering**.

Arches National Park, Utah

Weathering breaks rocks down into tiny bits. It turns big rocks into little rocks. It turns little rocks into sand.

It cuts tunnels through rocks. It carves rocks into strange shapes.

Erosion

What happens to all the bits made by weathering?

They often move from one place to another. Sometimes, the same substance that weathered a rock also moves it.

Rivers carry particles of rock, sand, and soil.

River

Oceans scoop up sand from one beach and dump it on another.

Wind blows rocks and sand.

Rocks big and small creep downhill. Sometimes they sweep downhill in an **avalanche**. Sometimes they are carried downhill and across the land by a **glacier**.

The movement of rocks, sand, and soil is called **erosion**.

Avalanche

Glacier

Mechanical Weathering

Have you ever found a rock that you could break in two? Then you have caused **mechanical weathering**.

Mechanical weathering changes the size or shape of a rock. It turns a rock into smaller bits. But the bits are not a new substance. They are still the same kind of rock.

Enchanted Rock State Park, Texas

Heating up by day and cooling off by night can weather a rock mechanically. The rock's outside **expands**, or grows bigger, in the heat of the sun. It shrinks at night. The outside of the rock heats and cools more quickly than the inside. This makes the rock crack and break.

A plant's growing roots can break apart rock, too.

Zion National Park, Utah

Water

A river or stream washes over rocks. It ripples around them. It also weathers and erodes them as it goes.

Ocean waves weather and erode rock as they smash into the shore. Water created this giant sea stack by wearing away the rock that connected it to the shore.

Haystack Rock at Cape Kiwanda, Oregon

A river or stream carries tiny bits of rock and sand in it. These bits scrape against rocks as they go by. They scrape off bits of the rock. Then the river may carry some of these bits away, too.

A river carved the Grand Canyon in Arizona out of rock. This canyon is a mile deep.

Grand Canyon, Arizona

Ice

Water also weathers rocks from the inside out.

Water trickles into cracks in the rock. It freezes inside the crack on a cold night, or in the winter. It turns into ice. When water turns into ice, it takes up more space. It expands. The ice pushes the crack a little farther apart. It makes the crack bigger.

Over time, more water trickles in. Water freezes and melts, over and over again, in the cracks. The cracks grow wider. Then chunks of rock split and fall off.

Bryce Canyon National Park, Utah

Glaciers

Glaciers are huge, slow-moving rivers of ice that creep like giant bulldozers down mountains and across land.

About 18,000 years ago, giant glaciers spread across North America and Europe.

They scooped up rocks and soil and carried them along. They scraped mountains that were in their way. They carved **valleys** and lakes.

Glacier National Park, Montana

Many of these glaciers are gone now. They melted long ago. But we can still see the weathering and erosion they left behind.

These glaciers flow slowly down Mount Rainier in Washington state.

Wind

Have you ever been on a sandy beach on a gusty day? The sand blown by the wind stings your skin.

Wind weathers rocks by blowing sand, too. It does not carry the sand very high, but it can drive the sand into rock with enough force to scrape and shape it.

Sand blown by the wind carved these rocks in the Western Desert of Egypt.

Wind also causes erosion. It makes sand form dunes that march across land. It can blow sand, soil, dust, or ash from a volcano for thousands of miles.

This rock in Antarctica was shaped by bits of windblown ice and rock.

Chemical Weathering

Weathering often does more than break rock apart. It can change rock into new substances. It can **dissolve** the minerals that hold a rock together. This is called **chemical weathering**.

Lichens and mosses that grow on rocks also make chemicals that can dissolve rock. This makes rock crumble.

Carlsbad Caverns, New Mexico

Rainwater has carbon dioxide in it. It can dissolve some kinds of rocks. This process forms beautiful caves underground in some places.

Weathering at Work

Sometimes, weathering and erosion cause problems.

Wind blows soil off farms. Floods of water wash away soil, too. They can make a hill fall apart in a mudslide. Weathering damages buildings, too.

We also need weathering and erosion. These forces shape the land. They make beaches. They even help make soil by crumbling rock into tiny particles of rock, sand, and clay.

Look around your neighborhood. Can you find any signs of weathering and erosion at work?

The sea eroded the beach around the Cape Hatteras lighthouse in North Carolina. In 1999, workers moved the lighthouse to keep it from falling into the ocean! The circle shows where the lighthouse was located.

Glossary

avalanche: snow, ice, rock, or dirt falling down a mountainside

chemical weathering: weathering that changes rock into a new substance

dissolve: blend in with water

erosion: the moving of rock, sand, and soil by water, wind, and ice

expands: grows larger

glacier: a slow-moving, thick river of ice

mechanical weathering: weathering that breaks and crumbles rock

valleys: dips in the land that lie between areas of higher ground

weathering: the crumbling and breaking of rock caused by water, wind, ice, heat, cold, plants, and chemicals